Inspirational Verse for Those Who Hunger and Thirst

A Book of Poems to Feed the Soul

By
Artemis Craig

Artemis Craig Publishing
Birmingham, Alabama

The opinions expressed in this manuscript are solely the opinions of the author. The author has represented and warranted full ownership and/or legal right to publish all the materials in this book.

Inspirational Verse for Those Who Hunger and Thirst
All Rights Reserved.
Copyright © <2013> Artemis Craig
1-941757160

Library of Congress Control Number: 2013917027

This book may not be reproduced, transmitted, or stored in whole or in part by any means, including graphic, electronic, or mechanical without the express written consent of the publisher except in the case of brief quotations embodied in critical articles and reviews.

Artemis Craig Publishing
http://wwwartemiscraigpublishing.net

ISBN: 978-0-9890876-0-5

PRINTED IN THE UNITED STATES OF AMERICA

Dedicated to:

Roderic Jernigan Jr., my son, and to Evangelist Sadie Craig and Clifford Craig Sr., my parents, who have always inspired me to make things better.

Speak Now

A lifetime passed before my voice was found,
It's hard to pinpoint exactly when I lost the sound.
Locked in a world where I screamed and no one heard,
I never offered anyone an encouraging word.

For all the times I held my peace, it's time to speak now
To tell some tormented misunderstood soul how
Much power there is in the spoken word
But you must choose to let your voice be heard.

Without words I became invisible which was fine by me,
Found a home for my anger and bitterness in my invisibility.
Disappointment and hatred festered inside all the while,
But none knew because through it all I wore a smile.

For all the times I held my peace, it's time to speak now
About the dark places I've been and proclaim discovery
Of a brand-new and improved me, and how
The sound of my voice has become
Instrumental in my recovery.

For all the times I've held my peace,
It's time to speak of a new phase,
To help someone see that trouble doesn't last always.
Don't spend another minute going through life
In a distorted haze
For your dreams can soar to wherever
You set your gaze.

Where Dreams May be Found

A dream is the wish your heart makes
On the hope it will come true,
Fulfillment of that dream is the action the body takes
To face all of the obstacles it has to go through.
Like shaking a nation free of racial prejudice,
Traveling through the hallowed halls of space
Extending the life of those who lay dying
Or to share with the world
The power of God's saving grace.

Dreams are not only found in a cozy bed
On a pillow beneath a sleeping head
You can find them in the graveyard
Buried forever among the cold and the dead.
Jesus spoke of a servant given a talent
Which he spitefully hid,
Unwilling to increase his master's money
As his fellow servants did.
For his treachery he lost his talent
To another already with ten
To be cast into outer darkness
Quicker than his head could spin.

Not unlike talent,
In the most inconspicuous places
Dreams may be found,
And like talent
They were never intended to wind up underground.
The only thing worse than wasted talent
Is unrealized dreams,
Or at least that's the way it seems.
So talented soul, please don't take your dreams
To the grave with you,
And miss out on the chance
Of being able to help make
Someone else's unrealized dreams come true.

Acknowledgement:

Thank you, Jesus, the author and finisher of my faith, from whom all blessings flow.

Special thanks to my sister Cyreatha (Nikki) and my brothers Clifford Jr., Timothy Sr., Carlton, Marquis, Bryce, Elgardo, and Steven.

People used to laugh at us for being our own baseball team, but by the grace of God, we're still together, loving and taking care of one another. For that, I am extremely grateful.

Also, thank you so much to my sisters Daisy, JoAnn, Lavoria, and my nephew Daniel, who lifted up my hands when they got weary while my mother was dying. To those of you who loved Mommy and helped me with her care, I say, "Many Thanks and Much Love."

Thank you to Karen Bishop, my best friend; Charles Bumpus, who reminded me that I was a poet and that I needed to see myself as such; Natalie Daniels, with whom I've shared many a quiet moment by the water where I found peace; and Phillip and Tina Craig and baby Christian, who were an inspiration to me in bringing this book to life.

I would also like to acknowledge my "Mini Me," Chante' Smith and her brother Tim Jr., and Roychelle who I depended on when I needed medical advice.

Lastly, I would like to say, "Thank you!" to the entire Craig Family who have toiled in the struggle with me for a very long time. Much Love to My Peeps…

Foreword

Facing adversities and coming out of the fire have made me stronger and allowed me the opportunity to encourage the hearts of those who are searching for something better. If you hunger and thirst for the part that's missing in your life, your spirit needs to be fed just like your body does. Fortunately, the bread of life falls from heaven to feed the souls of mankind to increase their faith, for everyone has a measure of faith. When this faith is acted upon, it can move moutains and cast them into the sea.

The poems you are about to read relates events in my life that describe my influence by strong women of God who wanted me to be saved. I was brought up reading stories from the Bible which I loved so much that I put them to lyrical verse.

Losing my way after the death of my grandmother and my father led me to a dark, silent place, but I was inspired to find my voice by writing poems that reconnected me with those strong women of God. The end of the book is a compilation of works inspired by the courage of persons who have overcome insecurities, life's obstacles, survived diseases, and incredible losses. I applaud them for their courage and strength to continue to fight and help someone else see that "I made it, and you can make it too!"

When life was darkest for me, I wrote poems to honor these people, both past and present, who have given me the courage to publish the poems I'd written as an anthology to pay homage to my mother's (Pentecostal) and my grandmother's (Baptist) teachings. I grew up Baptecostal and proud.

The poems *Speak Now* and *Where Dreams May be Found,* bear witness to my recovery as a work in progress and are therefore written separate from the listed works.

List of Poems

Baptist Fruit

Jewel of My Heart

You Are What You Eat

Southern Fried Soul Food

An Issue

Coat of Many Colors

City of Angels

Misery Seeks Comfort

Beyond Supping at the Feast

Inspirational Verse for Those Who Hunger and Thirst

The Flavor of Pentecost

Acts Two Thirty-Eight

Faithful Warrior

All in the Name

Later Than You Think

Sincere Prayer

Sacrifice of Blood

Quest for Fire

In Remembrance

Cut from the Pattern

Done in the Dark

Deep South Chow Chow Relish

Once More Tested

Life Not Mine to Save

A Way Out

Being "There"

Beneath a Star

Help Me to Hold Out

Bread of Life

A Place Alone I Could Go

A View at Twilight

Moment of Epiphany

Live the Dream

At First Sight

Royal Birth

Multitude of the Redeemed

See, Here Is Water

One Plants, One Waters, God Gives Increase

Dividing the Darkness

Wind of a Storm

Ode to Bishop Bumpus

A Ripple on the Water for Mom and Karen

A Woman of Substance

Give Thanks

Celebrate God's Goodness

Room for My Gift

Such as I Have I Give Thee

Baptist Fruit

With pen in hand I wrote out the stories in rhyme,

Granny, thank you for the precious time.

You taught me the power of God was right,

The way would not be easy; sometime I would have to fight.

Get the message out at all cost I must do,

In my own way to somehow repay you

For all the love and trust you had in me

Accept these poems as my gifts for others to see

And taste the fruit of your legacy.

Jewel of My Heart

Like a stone creates a ripple in still water
Josephine forever changed the lives of her sons and daughters.
Her hands possessed such strength, yet were so loving,
Whenever she planted seeds in the garden
Or put pies in the oven.
Working at her loom sewing a quilt for my bed,
Holding me in her arms, wiping the tears that I shed.
Jewel of my heart, I miss your voice soft as down,
Its timbre filled the house with melodious sound.
As you sang praises to our Savior all through the day,
You remind me forever with the Lord to stay.
As I gaze out over the waves on the Chesapeake Bay,
The jewel of my heart glistens in my mind in the most
Beautiful way.
I am reminded of sitting beside her on long bus rides,
To the home church in the country
A place reminiscent of happier days
Of morning worship and evening praise
Moments in time that sadly rolls away on the evening tide.
Love for God and my fellow man I learned at her knee,
The power of prayer and the secrets of fasting
She passed on to me.
I miss her wisdom in times of crisis and doubt,
That's when I try to be more like her and trust that from the
Darkness of the depths the Savior is faithful to bring me out.

This poem is dedicated in loving memory of Mrs. Josephine Thomas, the greatest grandmother this side of heaven. I'll see you again someday, Sweetheart.

You Are What You Eat

Grits, hash taters, thick-sliced bacon with pecan pancakes,
These can never be considered as one of life's great mistakes.
Alone or together, they're comfort foods
With rewards to the taste,
If eaten in excess they can be damaging to your natural man
Servings should be monitored with all haste.
Sins that can lead to spiritual death are sloth and gluttony,
I learned at a young age in the kitchen of my wise old granny.

"Be careful," she said, "everything you eat
May not be good for you,"
So eat faith and let your righteousness shine through.
Bread from heaven can be fulfilling when eaten by the slice,
It can keep your spiritual man healthy and free from vice.

Let it be said that you eat to live and not live to eat.
While still a suckling be satisfied with milk and not crave meat,
The food the world offers can leave you filled with pain,
Guard your soul in your efforts, the whole world to gain.
Sage advice from a woman
Who loved me more than her own life,
A woman determined to keep me from pain, misery, and strife.

"Everything you eat can't be good for your soul," I was told,
The cares of life can weigh you down and hinder your goal.
Bread from heaven can be fulfilling when eaten by the slice,
Your spiritual man gains strength through fasting
You'll see how much as you heed my advice.

Southern Fried Soul Food

Finger licking fried chicken, so good I chewed on a bone,
While Granny would tell me how
God would never leave me alone
To face life on my own
But would always provide tender loving care.
According to Granny, God would always be there
Faithful to show up when I was filled with despair.

She made sweet corn with bacon, the thick kind,
My mouth waters even now when I think of how
I crunched on the rind.
Back in the day with Granny making sure
The corn didn't scorch or burn,
While I listened to her stories from the Bible
That I eventually learned
And appreciated enough to put them to rhyme,
So that I could cherish them as something
We shared as a moment in time.

I can remember her theory that a person's soul needed to be fed,
Without reading the Bible, prayer, and having faith,
A soul would wind up dead.
Granny told me that God showed his love to us through deeds
He wanted us to do the same,
To do that we needed to exercise our faith
We need to believe in miracles
That had been performed in his name.

Granny warned me to keep God in my business
If I wanted to succeed,
And I believed just like her Southern fried
Soul food satisfied my natural hunger
I could find in God's Word everything on which
My spirit needed to feed.

Stories I learned in my grandmother's kitchen . . .

My granny told me stories from the Bible like the woman with the issue of blood and Joseph who was sold into Egypt to save his family and the blind man who received his sight. Each of them was faced with obstacles that tested their faith and put them in harm's way. Their tenacity inspired me as a child and even today.

An Issue

Searching for relief from her issue of blood,
That rained from her body in a constant flood.
The woman was desperate and at her rope's end,
All of her resources had been depleted on physicians
Leaving her with nothing left to spend.

As Jesus and his disciples passed nearby,
She purposed in her heart that she would live and not die.
Belief that a cure for her disease
Rested with this charismatic man,
She overcame all obstacles and stretched out her hand.
One touch to the hem of his garment stanched the awful flow,
That for twelve years caused her considerable misery and woe.

But her healing did not go unnoticed
Even though there was a crowd,
"Who touched me?" questioned Jesus who cried aloud.
The disciples were amazed
Jesus expected the guilty to confess,
When all around was such a great press.
"I felt virtue leave from me,
Who dares to receive my gift and quietly flee?"
Seeing that she could not hide
The woman came to Jesus with trembling, all aquiver.
Expecting a sentence of death from his lips he would deliver.
Instead, he told her, "Daughter, your faith has made you whole,
Go now on your way courageous and bold."

Coat of Many Colors

Joseph was born to Jacob in his old age
The boy brought his father joy and was dear to his heart,
Jacob made Joseph a coat of many colors to set him apart
From his brothers who thought of him as a dreamer.
In his heart he secretly desired
To someday have rule over them.
Among the brothers this caused discord
This made them jealous of him.

His brothers' jealousy proved to be cruel as the grave,
But God preordained that Joseph would be saved
From those who desired to bring an end to the dream
That God had.
In his infinite power God made for Joseph's good what
His brothers meant for bad.

Joseph was sold into Egypt, and his coat of many colors
Brought back to his father as evidence he would never return.
Hurt and confused the meaning of his dreams
Joseph had yet to learn.
He gained favor while in prison where he'd been placed
After being falsely accused of lying with Potiphar's wife,
His master's woman meant him harm,
But positively changed his life.

Released from prison by interpreting Pharaoh's dreams
Joseph's coat of many colors was replaced in his heart
With fine raiment and jewels which Pharaoh deemed
Necessary for someone of his newly appointed station,
For Joseph possessed the qualifications
Required to rule a nation.

Second only to Pharaoh throughout the land
Joseph became well respected and proclaimed "The Man"
Picked to deal uprightly in Egypt
In the time of want and in plenty,
Dishonesty in his dealings,
None could find any.

When the famine that was foretold
In Joseph's dream ravaged Egypt
Even encompassing the cities nearby,
The people in their suffering sent up a woeful cry.
Jacob asked his sons to visit Egypt to buy corn,
Joseph recognized his brothers
And was left shattered and torn.

News of his father and his youngest brother Benjamin
Brought tears to Joseph's eyes.
This he bore in secret for in his brothers' Presence
Joseph wore a disguise.
Joseph demanded Benjamin be brought to him
This against Jacob's desire,

Posing as an Egyptian, Joseph held Judah,
His older brother, captive
Inevitably his release would require that Jacob relent.
With great trepidation Benjamin was sent
To his brother who fell on his neck and they both wept,
As Joseph revealed his identity, a secret he'd solemnly kept.

In Egypt, Jacob was reunited with the son
He thought was long dead,
There was great rejoicing and many tears were shed.
For the dream that God had for Joseph was brought to light,
In the end, all was revealed and
A terrible wrong was put right.

City of Angels

Came to the City of Angels to find love,
Ended up having to rise above
The fear that I would not succeed,
But I never forgot Granny's advice about avarice and greed.
Got accepted into the University of Southern California Film School,
I studied with top filmmakers which felt pretty cool.
God was good, I was on my way,
To have the world hear what I had to say.
City of Angels, land of opportunity,
Be a map and show me
The way paved to fortune and fame,
Make it soon while I'm at the top of my game.
Doors opened quickly in the film industry,
I learned my craft and couldn't wait to see
The lengths I would have to go to make a movie.
Granny was elated at the news that I was doing well,
She always knew my grades before I had a chance to tell.
City of Angels, land of opportunity,
Stretched out before me, my future I clearly see.
Be a ray of sunshine shining bright,
Lead me to the place closest to heaven's light.
Just as things seem to fall into place,
I ended up going to a very dark place.
Granny was taken in the dead of night,
I didn't get to say good-bye and that was far from right.
We had been separated by two thousand miles.
I would have done anything for one of her smiles
For a single moment to help wipe away my tears,
And encourage me like she'd done for so many years.
City of Angels, land of opportunity,
The place where I searched for ways to be free,
I'm blinded by pain, my way I can hardly see,
Be an ocean and let me drown my sorrow in thee.

Misery Seeks Comfort

Misery seeks comfort after the devastating blow,
Of losing the pitch to Columbia executives
She'd just blown her first chance at the Big Show.
The degree of her pain could not be measured in size,
As the words "No Way in Hell" reflected in their eyes.
The sound of her grandmother's voice spoke softly in her ear,
To encourage Artemis with words she longed to hear.
"Nothing makes a failure but a trial
In that there is no shame,
All is not lost; don't let your heart be eaten up with blame."
Her granny's death was too fresh and she had not yet grieved,
Unfortunately her inconsolable sobs could not be retrieved.
What the executives thought was passion unbound,
It turned out to be Artemis's total emotional breakdown.
Misery needed comfort as she watched her career
Take a downward spiral,
And come to an end quicker than a YouTube video goes viral.
Sadly she perpetuates the cycle of despair
That epitomizes her name,
Desire for comfort for a moment
Dulls the pain of lost fortune and fame.
Misery loves comfort and seeks after it
In the most unusual places,
She finds it in the arms of a stranger
Who shows no traces
Of regret as he weaves a web of deception
And casts his net
To win her heart in a sucker's bet.
Their union was doomed and quickly fell apart,
But Artemis walked away to make a fresh start.
She held in her arms her greatest production, her life's joy,
And found the comfort she sought in
The smiles of her baby boy.
The highway stretched before her
Driving across country in her car,
Artemis waved good-bye to Misery
Also to her chances of shining like a star.
Headed back to Alabama where it all began,
Artemis tried desperately to find footing in quicksand.

Beyond Supping at the Feast

After being baptized into the body I was not satisfied
Being happy that I was spared the death that Jesus died
When the feast of the Lord was spread
I dared not completely partake,
I became filled with pride instead.
In my head thoughts like *Better him than me,*
Floated at will untethered — allowed to roam free
To eat my fill of everything my heart desired,
From the devil's lies and cunning I was most inspired.
Since that fateful day I've feasted
On confusion, despair, and doubt,
Supped with demons in pits from which I couldn't get out
Got a belly full of garbage that refused to digest,
Learned how to live with it and tried to do my best
To make others understand that I just wanted to be me,
Stop trying to put me in that box — let me be free!
Time passed and I was able to get beyond
My days of living like a vagabond
Life happened to teach me a thing or two
Unfortunately some of the lessons
Have only been learned by a few
Lost my invitation,
But showed up with the rest of the guests
Broken, downtrodden, my sins ready to confess.
I was okay with the crumbs that fell to the infidel
Gratitude for forgiveness is the story I now tell
Got a second chance and have no intentions to blow it
Wherever I go born-again believer
I'll claim and you better know it.

A New Chapter in My Life . . .

I started a new chapter in my life. I was home with my mother and I kept myself busy providing a life for my baby. I tried desperately to shake off my postpartum depression. It was hard, but I had the support of my family. I acknowledged there was problem when one night I called my mother from Los Angeles and told her that I was in trouble and had almost hurt my son because he wouldn't stop crying. She told this to my dad who told her to go to Los Angeles to get me. My mother and my sister, Nikki, drove the two thousand miles to bring me and Jay back to Birmingham.

In Birmingham, I couldn't sleep so my therapist kept upping the dosage on my meds until I told him I was sleeping even though I wasn't because the pills were making me hallucinate and wake up in places and not know how I got there. I had my wakeup call when I realized it was too dangerous waking up in an intersection with cars honking, angry drivers yelling, and my three-month-old baby asleep through the whole thing in the backseat. I took myself off the meds and went back to what I knew – church.

Inspirational Verse for Those Who Hunger and Thirst

For Those who hunger and thirst after righteousness
There is food for your soul
Which only through the body of Christ can you be made whole.
We take of his flesh and his blood in remembrance
During holy communion,
Longing for the day of our foretold glorious reunion.
He fed the multitude with fishes and loaves as the bread of life,
On calvary for our sins living water rained from his side
When pierced with a knife.
As manna from heaven the bread of life falls
Upon the water and washes up on the shore,
To feed those who diligently seek until they want no more.

The Flavor of Pentecost

Your life was proof that the doctrine of Pentecost
Can preserve and protect.
I watched you so many times as you would neglect
Your wants and desires as you preferred another,
While you labored in the vineyard amongst your
Sisters and brothers in Christ you found a savior,
You wanted the same for me.
Thank you so much, Mommy
Because of you, Jesus' light I can clearly see.

Acts Two Thirty-Eight

If there was a formula to get to heaven wouldn't that be great?
Well, there is, and it's found in Acts Two and Thirty-Eight.
Repent everyone in the name of Jesus Christ
The verse clearly states.
And receipt of the gift of the precious Holy Ghost
Shall be your wondrous fate.
A keeper from sin and comforter in dark hours,
The heat from God's spirit warms the body and soul
When it showers,
Down on the recipient who can't help but give vent,
With shouts and utterance in other tongues
Until their body, in sweet release, is spent.
Repentance and water baptism in Jesus' name
Is the key to open heaven's gate.
Baptized believers, now that you know the secret
It is your duty to proclaim to all you meet the words
Found in Acts Two and Thirty-Eight.

Faithful Warrior

A warrior stepped onto the shore of the Dark Continent
With only a Bible in her hand,
Equipped with a measure of faith she was determined
To make a stand
Accompanied by her pastor and fellow delegates,
Each of them well aware
That tenuous at best were their fates.
Undaunted by the sounds of the witch doctor's ravings,
The souls of idol worshipers were at stake
And in need of saving.
Faced with different dialects
As a language barrier to tear down,
The warrior depended upon
The voices of others in their midst
To bring the group to a place of middle ground

The man of God preached fire from heaven as in the latter rain,
To burn away the remnants of the idolater's sinful stain.
When the Holy Ghost fell upon them
Like on the Day of Pentecost

All reservation of salvation among them was lost.
The interpreters grew silent as the crowd yelled,
"We no longer have need of you.
Each in our native tongue hears this man's words to be true."

"See, here is water, what hinders you?" is what they heard,
They were pricked in their hearts from the spoken word.
That day two hundred souls were immersed
In the Atlantic deep
In God they placed their confidence.
As promised they received the precious gift of the Holy Ghost,
And spoke with other tongues as evidence.

My mother Evangelist Sadie Craig visited Liberia, West Africa, where she helped baptize souls into the apostolic faith. So proud of you, Mommy. So Much Love!!!!

All in the Name

I'd been praying for an answer to what I should do,
To get out of the tribulation I was going through.
The end of the tunnel was nowhere in sight,
I'd grown weary from crying myself to sleep at night.

A Holy Ghost-filled sister came and witnessed to me,
Baptized in Jesus' name, she said, is what you *MUST* be.
Well, I tried being a good Christian once or twice before,
Didn't find what I was looking for, and couldn't see myself
Going down that road anymore.

The name of the Lord is a strong tower,
The righteous run into it and are safe,
The sister said with great conviction,
Precious heart, salvation is the answer
For your suffering condition.

The Holy Ghost is that of which you are of most in need,
Call upon Jesus; he will come with all haste and speed
Bringing with him comfort and the ability to sooth all doubt,
And protect you from your enemies encamped round about.

Mommy was persistent, I had to give her that much,
The spirit of the Lord down on the inside put her in touch
With the pain and despair I was feeling
God gave her the words to let me know how to get my healing.

It's all in the name; Jesus has everything you need,
When it's your turn to sow a soul-winning seed
Graciously remember to do all in the name of
The Lord Jesus, whatsoever you do in word or deed.

Later Than You Think

To Those Unsaved...
Searching everywhere for rest for your soul,
You try to find the piece that can make you whole.
The answer is in Jesus, who gave his life on the cross,
To redeem sinful man who was destined to be lost.
Coming over to the Lord's side is a decision which has
You ever teetering on the brink.
Don't take too long in thought; it's Later than you think.

To Those Trying to be Saved...
Taking upon you Jesus' yoke and learning of his righteousness
You gain stamina through faith to face Life's tests.
Fear not to be the vessel of God's own hand,
Gather fortitude from within and boldly take a stand.
Be of good courage to do the Father's will,
As the crimson flood flows, let your heart be filled.
But don't waste too much time contemplating
Whether or not to drink,
Hasten now to take up your cup; it's later than you think.

To Those Once Saved . . .
Forgetting your first love and relinquishing your vow,
You promised to trust the Lord and shout hallelujah anyhow.
When storms come and press against your soul,
And you're in need of an anchor to grab ahold.
Resisting the shepherd's call attempting to make
It on your own,
To have your efforts leave you sad and feeling alone.
You're drowning in quicksand, and you're as deep
As you can sink,
Return to the sheepfold quickly,
It's later than you think.

To Those Who Regret Not Being Saved...
Missing the rapture and seeing Jesus' face,
After waiting for so long would be a terrible disgrace.
Hearken now to the Lord's sweet voice,
Don't take too long to make the right choice.
Take up the way of holiness; tout God's praises to all men,
Remain steadfast, refusing to take down, be not easy to bend.
Jesus makes ready the honeymoon for his bride,
That she might share his majesty and reign by his side.
For soon to come, even quicker than your eyes can blink,
Our time is not long; it's later than you think.

Sincere Prayer

A Sincere Prayer touches Heaven above,
In answer God Showers down his Blessings of Love.
Upon the Righteous willing to wait,
Not believing in luck, chance, or fate.
But trusting in the Word which keeps us on course,
Strengthening us against Satan's driving force.
It might take time for your request to sink in
But before you let the devil win, go back and pray again.

I was inspired to write the following poems as I tried to be saved . . .

Sacrifice of Blood

The soul that sins shall surely die,
Painful reckoning waits for them by and by.
To reverse the curse a bargain must be made,
A blood sacrifice was the price to be paid.
No longer acceptable, the flesh of goats and bulls,
Heaven's chosen was needed as debt paid in full.
The Lamb of God unselfishly lay his life down,
Led to the slaughter scourged and bound.
To a cross on Golgotha's lonely hill,
Jesus bore man's pain of his own free will.
By the tearing of his flesh we are sanctified,
Through the shedding of his blood, believers
Will never be denied
The opportunity to be at one with the Father
Bought back from sinning
Reclaimed to his rightful place,
As it was In the Beginning.

Quest for Fire

Before the dawning of time there was God,
In God's infinite wisdom it pleased God to create man,
In God's creating, God designed an intricate plan.
Paradise lost, searched for, and found,
For man and woman, immortality and sweet
Peace will abound.

Man, a needful creature, spends his entire life,
Attaining respect, wealth, offspring, and a loving wife
Always possessing a burning desire to attain more,
So close to opening the ever-elusive final door
As the nights grow long and the comforts grow few,
Man desperately atones, "Reveal to me your will, Father,
What is it that I must do?"

God's answer to man is easy to define,
It has dwelled with man since the dawn of time.
"Come to the fire, my son, it will give you light,
From its ashes, a garment snowy white,
Purging your soul to the very core,
Bringing forth strength and all good qualities that I adore."

Man in his own wisdom desires fire for comfort and sight,
Also to ward off creatures of the night
In man's search for fulfillment of his fleshly desire,
He is drawn, not of his own will, on a quest for fire.
God meekly offers him the ultimate comfort in the
Person of himself, the Precious Holy Ghost,
The heat from God being what man fears the most.

Shunning the watery grave prepared from the beginning,
Man tries to escape baptism in Jesus' name
To be free from sinning
For man must be born of the water
To receive the fire that burns within
That will purge his dark soul from past sin.
Man, a creature desiring to shape his own destiny,
Must learn to depend on God; a higher authority.

God's answer to man shall remain the same,
As God calls to every man by name
"Come to the fire, my son, it will give you light,
From its ashes, a garment, snowy white,
Purging your soul to the very core,
To bestow upon you, a new life like never before."

This was the first Christian poem I ever wrote to read aloud in church. That was almost twenty years ago. It's still one of my favorites. My grandmother never got to hear me recite it, but I'm sure she would have enjoyed it.

In Remembrance

Unclean, unworthy, and hidden from sight,
Until Jesus passed and witnessed
We were not many, numbering only ten,
We considered ourselves honest, yet leprous men.
Upon lifting our voices for mercy to be granted,
Instantly a seed of faith was planted.
None other could end our suffering and shame,
Or present us to the Father free from blame.
The scourge that ate away our flesh to the bone,
At Jesus' spoken word was immediately gone.

Jesus of Nazareth, please be merciful unto me.
I kneel in awe of this man from Galilee.
Came the words from the single leper healed of the ten,
He fell on his face and glorified God to no end.

"What of the nine?" was Jesus' reply.
"Did they not receive my virtue as I passed by?"
This is repayment for a kindness given freely,
The son of man cannot easily deny his destiny.
Not my will, but my Father's will for me,
That I accursed must hang from a tree.
To pay a sin debt of which I took no part,
I dared not refuse because of man's closeness to my heart.
Jesus of Nazareth, show thy mercy unto me,
"We kneel in awe of this man from Galilee"
Comes the words from baptized believers
Cleansed from Adamic stain,
As they remain in remembrance of sin's dreadful pain.

Cut from the Pattern

One Day a Tailor Came From Heaven
And Gave Up the Right of His Birth,
To Design a Pattern for Those of Us on Earth
For His Clothing He Searched Thru Fine Fabrics
Including Lace and Sheer Mesh,
He Was Suited Best in a Robe of Flesh.
Although His Beginnings Were Humble and Low,
He Graciously Invited All Men to Follow on to Know
That Prayer Is a Desire Expressed to God in Word,
Along with Fasting Man's Desires Can Be Heard.
Worshipping the Father with Praise and Thanksgiving,
He Thus Perfected the Pattern in Everyday Living.
His Garment of Holiness Was the Height of Fashion
The Apostles Grew Strong in Faith and Spread
The News of His Power with Joy and Great Passion.
Alas, the Time Came When the Tailor Had to Say Good-bye,
To Regain His Heavenly Birthright, He Had to Die.
He Left Behind a Book Called the B.I.B.L.E.
As a Point of Reference for You and Me for What It's Worth,
As <u>B</u>asic <u>I</u>nstructions <u>B</u>efore <u>L</u>eaving <u>E</u>arth.
Today We Continue in the Way of the Apostles
Doctrine Practicing Fellowship
And the Breaking of Bread,
Like Jesus before Us, Ensuring That
Hungry Souls Be Fed.
He Shall Return as Promised Looking for a Church
Cut by the Pattern He Himself Laid,
Let Us Rejoice in Him and Be Glad for We Are
Cut from the Pattern That God Made.

Done in the Dark

To follow Jesus' pattern I did my best,
I was constantly being put to the test.
Asked myself what would Jesus do?
Always answered the question with "to thine
Own self be true."

I was selfish in my so-called salvation
For that I would have to pay.
I made light of the Apostles' doctrine
That would bring a reckoning one day.

Mommy tried to prepare me — she offered to be my guide,
I failed again and again trying to come over to the Lord's side.
For most people to look at me
They would say that I finally got it right,
Looks can be deceiving
What's done in the dark will come to the light.

Deep South Chow Chow Relish

One part cut cabbage, one part chopped cucumbers
In scalding vinegar
With salt, paprika, and turmeric to amplify the flavor,
You get Deep South Chow Chow Relish
A little something, something you can savor.
My mother took her time and cooked hers slow,
Twelve hours in the pot with the fire on low.

Chow Chow relish gives collard greens a bit of a kick,
Along with corn bread drizzled in melted butter,
Sliced extra thick.

Sadie was happiest when she served you a plate,
Her heart would smile as you sat and ate.
And relished the taste of the tangy dish she was famous for,
Cooking Chow Chow for her was never a chore.
The relish was likened to praise which brings God pleasure,
As a savory sweet he can treasure.

Chow Chow makes kale and turnips hit the spot,
It's perfect when you're looking for something spicy or hot.
With her Pentecostal experience
Sadie took the same special care,
Mommy knew the virtue of fasting and the power of prayer.
She would sing, "You're Gonna Need It Like the Bible Said,"

Each day that was the news she faithfully spread.
She would pray that a hunger for the Word of God
And a thirst for God's spirit
Would be a blessing
To anyone listening that was able to hear it.

Chow Chow relish brings to cabbage a touch of zing,
With a zest that makes the taste buds sing.

Mommy warned me that Satan would turn up the heat,
To test my faith through his wiles he would try to defeat.
My efforts to win the battle against his strongholds,
I would need the precious Holy Ghost to stir up the gift
That resides in me to stand firm and bold.
Unfortunately, I was unable to commit
I sat straddling the fence,
There was no way I would give up the life
I wanted to experience.

I continued to love Chow Chow
But never learned to make it,
I wanted Mommy to be proud of me
But I couldn't fake it.
Not unlike Chow Chow relish
As an additive that enhanced food's taste,
I ran from the Holy Ghost as a spiritual additive
For to live happy I had to get away
My exodus needed to be immediate
I had no time to waste.

Once More Tested

The test of Granny's love proved
She saw no fault in me,
Mommy's love revolved around the person
She thought I should be.
Even though I was far from perfect,
Daddy loved me unconditionally.
The test of my love for them
Showed me as wanting to have my own way,
I owed each of them a debt I could never repay.
I tried to be saved for Mommy's sake
Granny would have wanted it that way,
Daddy just wanted me in his life each day.
Went to church faithfully, God's Word to hear,
Couldn't wait until the preacher was finished
So I could quench my thirst with an ice-cold beer.
That was one test I failed miserably,
Nothing could prepare me for what I was yet to see.
Dressed up like the rest of the sisters
I passed myself off as a saint,
If they really knew the truth
Most of them would swoon — then faint.
The time would come when
I had to give up pretending I had the Holy Ghost,
And take my punishment for perpetrating a huge hoax.
I was once more tested — found myself caught in a lie,
My atonement was to watch the one who loved me die
In my arms which nearly cost me my sanity.
I had to be fixed — Help Jesus! Have mercy!

Life Not Mine to Save

One, one thousand, two, one thousand
Chest compressions like I'd been taught weren't enough
Formed a seal over your mouth and into it blew a quick puff.
Stay with me! Stay with me! But you refused to wake,
Over again, over again the previous steps I'd vainly take.
Panic crept stealthily up along my spine
Clinging to my will like a choking vine.
Fear gripped me at the thought of your smile
Being gone forever,
Broken was the promise that you would leave me never.
The air sucked out of the room along with your final breath,
My life filled with gloom as you traded your life for death.
The relationship between father and daughter had never
Been stronger,
Sadly we were not fated to have our bond last longer.
Our journey together ended and family told me to be brave,
Though it's hard to believe, your life was not mine to save.
Anger at God is all I can feel,
That along with the hope that somehow
This can't possibly be real.
You've gone on to a better place are words I don't receive
People ought to leave me alone while I grieve.
If I hear one more time, "I know what you're
Going through"
Don't judge me when I respond with, "How could you?"
Suspended in dark space filled with shame
Holding on to guilt for not saving your life
I feel I am to blame.
Away from me, Daddy, your body lies in the cold grave
It seems like only yesterday, try as I might,
Your life was never mine to save.
But mine to cherish in moments of panic and doubt,
To keep as memories when I feel trapped and can't get out.

Weight of the Clouds . . .

There were days when the clouds hung so low that I felt they would touch the ground and never let me up from under the weight that held my mind in a prison designed by the enemy, the father of all lies, who wished to have me. I was of two minds during this time. I wanted God to save me from myself and the bad decisions I was making because I believed that God could. But I also blamed God for not helping me when things went wrong and not coming to my rescue. I wasted so much time waiting on God to show up – only to realize that God had been waiting on me.

A Way Out
More pills, hallucinations, and lost memories
Filled my day,
It didn't seem to matter to anyone that
I no longer had much to say.
Lost in misery I quietly drifted away.

A blast from my past came back around,
Through our son we were intricately bound.
He offered me a way out of Birmingham city.
I jumped at the chance to wind up in a place without pity.

Besides snakes and scorpions down in that pit,
I found that I was made of true grit.
Things got intense, this much is true.
The next few poems are a testament to what I went through.

A Place of Desolation cannot be recognized if you have Never Found Yourself Being "There."

Being "There"

It's hard to understand the power of prayer,
Until you find yourself being "There."
In that period of storm where you're buffeted to and fro,
In desolation with no cell reception and surrounded by woe.
The prayers of the righteous avail much,

They soar to heights where only God can be touched.
No one knows the power of prayer,
Until they find themselves being "There."

You know the place I mean . . . In that place of despair,
Where nothing can help but a fervent prayer.
The place where your finances aren't worth a thin dime,
Where you're on your knees and have lost track of time.
The place where you felt you would never get back from,
That place where you thought love was afraid to come.

Someone fell on their face to God with you in mind,
Praying for God's peace that you might find.
For the prayers of the righteous avails much,
They soar to heights where Jesus can be touched.

Beneath a Star

Your hand of protection covers me
The nights I spend alone underneath a star,
Contemplating the heavens
From the backseat of my car
Making the most no matter the cost
Trying to salvage sanity from the things I've lost.

Your voice of encouragement speaks
To the ears of my soul,
Providing comfort and filling the gaping hole.
Left after my dreams escaped on the wind
Rending asunder the pieces of my mind,
In the wake of the carnage left behind.

Beneath a star where I resided in self-inflicted frequency,
I felt unworthy of anyone's help or sympathy.
Jehovah Jirah, you have been my provider
When my way was unclear,
Father, you alone my cry did hear.
Delivering my soul from the enemy,
Lighting my path so that I could see
Past the fear that paralyzed me.

The fire of your spirit sears my heart,
Numbing the pain so I can start
All over again and this time get it right.
Always warring, but never winning the fight.
My life in your hands is not easy to trust,
But laid bare and bereft, once again,
I find that in you I must.

Help Me to Hold Out

Lord, Help Me to Hold Out to My Last Dime,
Help Me So That I Won't Commit a Crime
And Sin against You
When You've Been Nothing but Good.
Step in, Jesus, and Fix It for Me Before
I Quit Believing You Could.
For Promotions I've been overlooked,
Times Taken for Granted Could Fill a Book.
Lord, Help Me to Hold Out
When Disappointment Is All Around,
Until the Time I Can Lift Up My Head
And Walk into My Blessings Free and Unbound.
Help Me to Hold out When I've Done All I Can Do,
In Times of Trouble, Lord, I Need a Word from You.
In You I Trust All My Needs to Supply,
Help Me, Father, Answer My Prayer By and By.
Lord, Help Me to Hold Out When the
Cares of My Life Take Precedence,
When My Faith in Your Voice I've Lost Confidence.
Help Me to Be More like Mary and Seek the Better Part
To Hold It Safely in My Heart
So I Can Sit at Your Feet and Learn Thy Ways,
From This Day Forward Until the End of My Days.

My Soul Hungers for Better Days . . .

I spent my time trying to make me get better by searching my soul for answers and finding strength in self-reflection down by the river where I found my voice.

After taking a good look in the mirror I saw the need to eat more of the bread of life through encouragement and less of the prescriptions that distorted my perception. It was critical for my spiritual man to receive nourishment for I found myself living in the land of "Want." I was searching for a dream, and in the meantime, I'd fed on carrion which rotted my insides. But by God's grace, I regained my appetite for the wisdom I received from my grandmother and my mother who taught me about life and introduced me to Christianity while serving up savory dishes of fried corn, okra, fried green tomatoes, collard greens smothered in Deep South Chow Chow Relish, along with bone-chewing fried chicken.

Bread of Life

In those days the multitude being very great,
To receive healing their numbers would not dissipate.
Jesus being compassionate noted the date,
He marveled that it had been three days since anyone last ate.
The disciples were forced to endure the crowd,
Send them away hungry they were not allowed.

Bread of Life, feed me until I want no more,
Let me enjoy the wonderful life for me you have in store.
Jesus asked the disciples how many loaves they had.
The answer was seven,
Jesus gave thanks and broke the bread
Which stretched like it was blessed from heaven.
Two small fishes the disciples found,
They set before the people as they sat on the ground.

Bread of Life, feed me with your strength and joy divine,
This I pray you as you continue to elevate my mind.
The story still resounds of the miracle that happened that day,
Four thousand ate before they were sent on their way.
Seven baskets full were recovered of meat and bread,
Jesus was the bread of life on which the hungry were fed.

A Place Alone I Could Go

"If you die, Granny, I'll die too,"
Weren't they the words I once promised you?
Unfortunately, in your final moments I was not there
To offer you comfort
Mine would not be the last words you would hear
Ambitious and bright, I was busy furthering my career.
As with all things, time passed, but the wounds did not heal,
Stubbornly I refused to accept your death as being real.
Alas, how did I wind up in this damnable state?
Using my words to fight off the urges to self-medicate
Or self-mutilate,
It's not just an escape from the negative emotions
That overwhelms me,
I write about the darkness to set the demons inside me free.
Before I even knew it began, it became a game to sit by the river
To ask the current where she'd been
While I contemplated her beautiful freedom
I would convince myself not to dive in.
Searching for a place that I alone could go,
I found my voice and let it flow.
Like the river along endless banks to cause ripples in time
As a stone causes ripples upon the water
That travels through my troubled mind.

A View at Twilight

*Here I am in the place where the world is blessed
With the moon's crystal light,
The place where the sun kisses the world good night.
The place between sunset and nightfall,
On my knees along the beach I crawl.
A sojourner in need of solace along with
Gilead's balm to soothe my hidden scars,
I hope to find a key to release my prison bars.
Searching for the way out of my darkened plight
Where for too long I learned to exist in twilight.*

*God witnessed my double life
And offered me a wonderful opportunity,
His sweet voice in the shadows whispered to me.
"Forgiveness of those who have done you wrong
Will cause your pain to come to an end,
Start now to let your journey to healing begin."
To his words in my heart as a planted seed,
I without hesitation took heed.*

*"I forgive you," words I offer to those at whose
Hand I suffered hurt and great despair,
I gladly recite as I lay my soul bare.
Bathed in heaven's light,
I no longer dwell in twilight.
Humbly I watch the day give way to night,
My heart swells like the waves as joy replaces spite.
As bitter gall disappears among the waves
Forever removed from my sight.*

Moment of Epiphany

My moment of epiphany came as I sat by the river,
I prayed to God my soul to deliver
From the chains in which I was bound.
I promised the Lord to be real this next time around.

In the river I found the peace I longed for among the waves,
There I resigned the bodies of Granny and daddy
To their graves.
After all, their spirits had always resided in me.
I'd wallowed in pity long enough
It was time to set their spirits free.

To soar to the sky and glow brighter than any star,
I knew they both wanted me to succeed and go far.
For that to happen I had to want it too,
It was up to me to put an end to what I was going through.
I desired another chance to change my fate,
Please, God, don let it be said that I was too late!

Not Too Late to Live the Dream . . .

I asked God to forgive me for being a fake and show me how to be happy. God spoke to me through someone who recognized my talent and showed me that I had a gift that would be a shame to waste. I gratefully embraced my gift. I also learned to forgive myself and listen to the sound of my own voice. Like Joseph in the story of the Coat of Many Colors, events changed the plans I had for my life, but in the end, I chose to live the dream that God had for me.

Live the Dream

Yours is a voice that speaks to the hearts of men,
To silence such a voice would be a terrible sin.
My answer was simple to my friend's insightful word
The most beautiful sound I'd ever heard.

Out of the mouths of two or three,
There is truth to what you say, I must agree.
My granny voiced the exact same words years before,
She calls to me now to walk through the open door.
My appointed time has come to fulfill the prophesy
In which I live the dream God has for me.

Connecting with My Faith . . .

When I had no idea where I was going I found it best to go to back to where I started from. I grew up in a family that knew quite a bit about faith and how to get a prayer through. When I'd tried everything else I grabbed hold to what was inside of me to light the way out of the dark place I'd slipped into. I embraced the soul food my mama and granny used to serve up back in the day and opened wide and took a big bite from the stories out of the Bible that I'd learned at their knee, giving the verses voice lyrically.

At First Sight

Who among us would gladly travel the earth?
Living as the man blind from birth,
Through no sin of his parents or of his own
The sightless man was destined to be healed,
To ensure that the works of his Heavenly Father
Would be revealed,
Jesus received his commission to work while it was yet day,
Night cometh and no man could work but should always pray.

The man's eyes Jesus anointed with clay
Which he commanded to wash away
In a muddy pool called Sent,
Although the request seemed foolish with his sight so close
In his efforts the man dare not relent.
At first glance, men as trees was what he saw,
Then the fog melted like a winter thaw.
He saw men as men for the first time to his delight,
When pointed out to the Pharisees by those who knew him
He readily admitted that on the Sabbath he received his sight.

Royal Birth

On a night much like tonight,
Our Savior's birth was heralded by starlight,
Jesus of Nazareth was born of royal birth,
Of the lineage of kings who roamed the earth.
Destined to die to save many nations,
He traveled down through forty-two generations.
Being the King of kings he laid aside his crown,
Upon coming of age he laid his life down.

His blessed shed blood was the cost to redeem all men,
A debt he willingly paid to cleanse away the blemish of sin.
We who are not worthy of such a gift,
Give thanks and his name do willingly uplift.
King of kings, Lord of lords, your name shall we exalt,
While we await Jesus' coming on that great day without
Blemish or fault.

Multitude of the Redeemed

Baptism of the body and renewing of the mind,
Are Essential to Salvation of the Souls of Mankind.
Seeking Diligently the Master's will,
Gaining Strength while Heavenly Goals they fulfill.
Born of the Water, Purged by the Fire,
To be molded in the Image of Jesus is their true Desire.
These are They whose Faith has been tried,
These are They whose Death Jesus Died.
These are They Redeemed under the Crimson Flood,
Their robes ever cleansed by the Savior's Precious Blood.

Before the Throne of the Lamb Wearing Robes of White,
Beholding God's Magnificence, His Power, and His Might
They cannot be counted their Number is so Great,
All worshipping the King of Glory; Accepting an Amazing Fate
To Share the Heavens with the Father of Creation Forever,
Basking in his love and satisfaction as God's greatest endeavor
These are they whose Faith has been proved,
These are they Like a Tree by the Waters that cannot be moved.
These are they Redeemed under the Crimson Flood,
Their robes ever cleansed by the Savior's Precious Blood.

Coming Out of Great Tribulation,
Enduring Hardships, Suffering, and Grave Degradation
Persecuted for Praising the Name of Jesus before Unbelievers,
Warring against the wiles of the devil's deceivers
 From All Nations and Languages
They'll gather on that Momentous Day
When the Lord Shall Give Comfort
And Banish All Their Fears Away.
These are they, who shall cry No More!
These are they who will walk boldly Through Paradise's Door.
These are they Redeemed under the Crimson Flood,
Their robes ever cleansed by the Savior's Precious Blood.

See, Here Is Water

See, here is water from it there should be no fear,
What holds you back from baptism in Jesus' name?
For newness of life awaits you here.
Therein salvation may be found,
Through burial beneath the waves
Awaits deliverance from past sins that had you bound
Repentance is necessary according to
Acts two and thirty-eight

As preached by the apostles of the past and present date.
See, here is water that can bring peace to your soul,
And also provide a majestic beauty for your eyes to behold.
Rise up as a blessed creature from the endless depths
Cleansed from shame,
To spread the Gospel of Jesus Christ who is faithful to
Present you before your Heavenly Father innocent of blame.

One Plants, One Waters, God Gives Increase

The death, burial, and resurrection of Jesus Christ
Is a story that for years has been retold
By blood-washed believers both young and old
Who labor as one body awaiting the day that Jesus
Splits the clouds to claim his church,
An event that has been the topic of much discussion
And endless research.
In the body of Christ there are many members
Working together in unison to grow crops of faith and hope
In the hearts of souls seeking peace,
One plants, one waters, and God gives the increase.
Each member from the moment
Into the body they are blood-born,
Has a specific task they are chosen to perform.
The Apostle Paul explained to the young church at Corinth
He was not meant to baptize, but was meant to preach,
Toward that goal he sought daily to reach.
Knowing that those in the vineyard would be rewarded
According to their labor,
With the edification of the body bringing about equal favor.
For in the body of Christ there are many members with
No vocation being separated in importance
From greatest to least,
To reap a soul harvest, one plants, one waters

— And God gives the increase.

Dividing the Darkness

Life is likened to a Light That Shines upon a Hill.
Dividing the Darkness of Man's Unconquerable Will
Born of the Water, Proven by the Fire,
To Glorify the Father Should Be Our Only Desire.
For the Light within Us Was Created by God's Design
As a Guide to Unbelievers to Illuminate Their Minds
Revealing to them, His Peace and Joy Divine.

Heaven is likened to a Place without Despair,
For There Shall Be No Sign of Nighttime There.
According to the book of Revelation,
They Shall Need No Candle
As They Gather From Every Nation.
For God Gives Them Light and That Light
Shall have the Light of Life
As a Beacon Worn by the Church, His Wife
To Help a Soul While They're Dividing
The Darkness in Their Life.

Wind of a Storm

Prayer is but a tender Planted Seed,
In Fertile Soil Blooming as God
Meets Us in the Midst of Our Need
Encouraging the Weak to Throw Off
Anchors and Divers Weights that hold them down,
Releasing Their Faith from Shackles
That had them bound.
Believers Should Forever Pray to Loose Satan's Grip,
Upon the Lives of Our Brethren Not Yet Equipped.

To stand victorious in spite of Stiff Opposition
And boldly Witness God's Promises come to Fruition.
Pray Without Ceasing, Jesus Will Hear,
As You Fight the Devil without Fear
Of Weapons against You, that He May Form,

On the Breath of a Lie or the Wind of a Storm
Bending One's Knee is Time Well Spent,
In the Presence of the Creator
Souls Are Free to Give Vent
To the Spirit that Dwells Within
To Guide Their Paths and Keep Them from Sin.

Words of Inspiration Are Needed When Your Soul Is Tested...

The sun does shine through the clouds.

The following poems were written to encourage persons who survived the loss of a loved one or went through a life changing experience that left them with personal hurdles to get over. These persons have been a source of inspiration to me because they did not give up when the question in their life was, "Why Me?" Some are still fighting for their lives yet keep in mind that the sun does shine through the clouds. Their faith is strong and for that they have my deepest admiration.

Ode to Bishop Bumpus

"A Place of Peaceful Serenity"
What do you say to someone who has lost a loved one so dear,
How can you help them see the end when the road is unclear?
By being there in Their Time of Sorrow,
Offering Assurance that there is Hope for Tomorrow.

Charles, remember the Spirit of the Lord is near,
To lift your Heavy Heart and Dry your Silent Tear.
And Meet You in A Place of Peaceful Serenity,
That place where Father and Son can Share a Special Memory.

In Praise to the Lord Raise Your Voice,
Join the Heavenly Host of Angels and Rejoice.
For now is not the time for sadness but the time to Celebrate,
To Be Present with the Lord Is a Joyous and Enviable Fate.

Bishop Bumpus let His Light among Men So Shine,
His Reward He Now Accepts as Peace and Joy Devine.
His Love for You is the Piece of Himself He Leaves Behind,
May You Cherish that Love and in it Comfort you'll find.

Never doubt the Spirit of the Lord so quiet and Serene,
As you sit and contemplate this Peaceful Scene.
And Remember the Moments with Your Father
That Meant So Much,
A Warm Smile from His Lips
From His Hands a Loving Touch.

A Ripple on the Water for Mom and Karen

Mom and Karen changed like the weather,
There were good times and bad times when
Those two got together.
Even though they didn't always see eye to eye,
Mom and Karen dared to try.
To be as close as a daughter and mother could,

Letting go of the bad and embracing the good
Accepting one another's differences and saying it's okay
Acknowledging how much they meant to each other
At the end of the day,
Sharing their expressions of love,
Each in her own way.

Memories of moments together
Will stay forever on Karen's mind,
To cherish as the special part of Mom that she left behind.
Like a ripple on the water transcending the distance
Of space and time,
Strengthening the bond between Mother and Daughter,
In the peace within that they both were able to find.

A Woman of Substance

I am known as many things in this life,

Friend, Lover, Mother, Wife.

Faith is the essence of my being,

It is the strength that keeps me going without seeing

My way through uncharted territory,

As I run headlong onto the battlefield,

I'm armed with sword, buckler, and shield

To wage war against the enemy who wishes

He was able to sift me as wheat.

Though I might be slain I shall never admit defeat

For I am a woman of substance,

Daughter of the Most High,

Putting the devil on notice that I shall not die,

But shall live and declare the works of the Lord.

This poem is dedicated to Patrice Ravizee as she awaits a donor to give her a kidney. Her faith is being tested which is a battle she will win.

Give Thanks

Give Thanks All Ye Redeemed of the Son of Man,
Lift Up Your Voices; Be Counted for Taking a Stand
Telling of Jesus' Marvels and Wonders,
His Timeless Creations Shall No Man Put Asunder.
Jesus' Love Is as Deep and Wide as the Sea,
His Power to Forgive Reaches Higher than the Tallest Tree.
Without a Doubt the Magnificence of His Esteemed Royalty,
Deserves Our Undying Pledge of Loyalty.
Lord, Thy Reverence Shall Always Be in the Praise
That I Sing to You for the Remainder of My Days.
My Help Cometh Only From Thee,
I Am Only Because You Allow Me to Be.
Give Thanks to the Lord Whose Spirit Dwells Within,
Keeping the Soul Desiring to Stand, Safe from Sin
Rejoice in His Blessings of Both Pleasure and Pain,
For This Is the Yardstick by Which to Measure
The Strength You Gain
Harden Not Your Heart While Going Through Your Test,
With Love and Diligence Give God Your Best.
Lord, Thy Reverence Shall Always Be in the Praise,
That I Sing of Your Blessings I've Seen in Countless Ways.
I Look to the Hills Daily from Whence My Help Abounds,
In Thanks, Hallelujah Is My Constant Joyful Resound.

Celebrate God's Goodness

Though God slay you in God will you trust,
He is ever faithful and always just.
To give you the desires of your tender heart,
Along with renewed strength to make a fresh start
So celebrate God's goodness with a Great Shout!!!
It's okay! Throw your head back and Let It Out!!!

Send your praise soaring on the farthest wind,
Toward the heavens to ascend
And return as a blessing none can measure,
Your Jordan to possess and forever treasure.

God has seen you suffer yet continue to pray,
For joy and peace on some sweet day
Take comfort and know that as
He provides for the fowl of the air,
Your Heavenly Father takes great care
To shoulder the load in your life
That you could never bear.

Room for My Gift

Blessed is the man who accepts his gift and allows it to grow,
He who does not is destined to be filled with a life of woe.
As in being stuck in a state of arrested development,
Instead of benefitting from blessings that have been heaven sent.
I never considered my ability to turn a phrase as anything
Other than something to do.
It's not hard to take for granted the things that come easily to you.

Lost sight of my gift and the fact that it was not mine to keep,
Somehow forgot how to dream even while I was asleep
Until a friend pointed out that poetry is an art
That we must continue to celebrate today.
Who better than a poet to find the words to say?
To encourage the soul who knows exactly how you felt,
While making the best of the hand you've been dealt.

After getting back in touch with my faith
I learned to dream again,
Finally understood the meaning of the words a man's gift
Makes room for him and brings him before great men.
In a moment Proverbs chapter eighteen verse sixteen
Made perfect sense.
So I dug through the boxes in the closet where my gift lay hidden,
Brushed away the dust from the pages I had once written,
And with God's help proceeded to get back my confidence.

Such As I Have I Give Thee

We are all endowed with gifts as we travel along day by day,
Not fully understanding their value until we give them away.
A man lame from his mother's womb
Was laid daily by the Beautiful gate,
Begging alms from passersby he remained in a pitiable state
Until one day he asked alms from Apostles Peter and John.
Imagine his shock when Peter replied
Silver and gold have I none.

But such as I have I give thee,
In the name of Jesus Christ of Nazareth you are free
To rise up and walk and forever tell the story
Of the wondrous gift you received to God's amazing glory.

The value of Peter's gift
Had to be more than the lame man bargained for,
Like many of us he was given the key to unlock his faith.
He boldly walked through the door
Of his dreams where he was made whole,
His feet touching the ground, heels, toes, ankles and sole.

It is a great pleasure to bestow a gift
That changes the life of the receiver,
As is in the case with Jesus and every blood-washed believer
These words, hungry soul, may not increase your wealth
Or even improve the quality of your health.

But such as I have I give thee,
In the name of Jesus Christ of Nazareth you are free
To share in the feast of the Lord and be made whole,
By quenching your thirst and satisfying your hunger
For his righteousness with this food for your soul

About the Author

Artemis Craig grew up the fourth of nine children to a steelworker father and educator mother in Birmingham, Alabama. Artemis developed a love for writing at an early age and wrote her first stage play at the age of nine. She graduated with a B.F.A. from USC Film School.

Her collection of poems, *Inspirational Verse for Those Who Hunger and Thirst* (2013) reflects her Baptist/Pentecostal roots where she uses lyrical poetry to inspire others to find their inner peace and strength through faith.

Presently, Artemis is finishing her first novel and developing film projects with Never Surrender Productions. She divides her time between Birmingham and Newport News, Virginia.

www.ingramcontent.com/pod-product-compliance
Lightning Source LLC
Chambersburg PA
CBHW041642090426
42736CB00034BA/13